SECRETS OF THE PLANT WHISPERER

How To Care For, Connect, And Communicate With Your House Plants

SECRETS OF THE PLANT WHISPERER

How To Care For, Connect, And Communicate With Your House Plants

S. F. Howe

Diamond Star Press
Los Angeles

Secrets of the Plant Whisperer: How to Care for, Connect, and Communicate with Your House Plants

Copyright © 2012 S. F. Howe
ISBN-10: 0977433501 (First Paperback Edition)

Second Edition © 2018 S. F. Howe
ISBN-10: 0977433587
ISBN-13: 9780977433582

Published by Diamond Star Press
Made in the United States of America

On behalf of the Green, and for the house plant lovers of the world without whom this book would never have been written

Books by S. F. Howe

MIND · BODY · SPIRIT

PLANT INTELLIGENCE

Secrets Of The Plant Whisperer
How To Care For, Connect, And Communicate With
Your House Plants

Your Plant Speaks!
How To Use Your House Plant As A Therapist!
Coming Soon!

HIGHER CONSCIOUSNESS

Matrix Man
How To Become Enlightened, Happy And Free In An
Illusion World

The Top Ten Myths Of Enlightenment
Exposing The Truth About Spiritual Enlightenment
That Will Set You Free!

The Bringer Discourses
On Waking Up To The Mind Control Programs Of The
Matrix Reality

PERSONAL GROWTH

Vision Board Success
How To Get Everything You Want With Vision Boards!

Sex Yoga
The 7 Easy Steps To A Mind-Blowing Kundalini
Awakening!

Morning Routine For Night Owls
How To Supercharge Your Day With A Gentle Yet
Powerful Wake-up Routine!

CONSCIOUS HEALTH

When Nothing Else Works
How To Cure Your Lower Back Pain Fast!

Transgender America
Spirit, Identity And The Emergence Of The Third Gender

Free Gift

As my thanks to you for reading *Secrets of the Plant Whisperer: How to Care for, Connect and Communicate with Your House Plants,* I would like you to have the gift of a starter library containing two special ebooks, "The Art of Bonsai" and "A Beginner's Guide to Organic Vegetable Gardening."

These ebooks open the door to completely new arenas of plant care. I'm so excited to think about how you can apply the secret knowledge you acquire from *Secrets of the Plant Whisperer* to growing beautiful bonsai trees or tasty organic vegetables!

To receive your free gift, just send an email to info@diamondstarpress.com with your purchase receipt and 'Send Plant Whisperer Gift' in the subject field, and we will get your free gift out to you right away. Do it now, before you forget!

Table of Contents

Preface

Science and Plant Intelligence

Before we explore in depth the mindset and practices of a plant whisperer, let us consider the scientific evidence for plant intelligence. This chapter presents an overview of some of the remarkable research findings in the areas of plant awareness and plant intelligence, along with a list of recommended online sources.* If you enjoy learning about this subject, those web pages and websites are an excellent place to further your studies.

Many of you will find it easier to relax and 'enjoy the flight' after your logical mind has been assuaged by the scientific facts. But for those who just want to get on with it – please proceed directly to the next chapter, "Introduction to The Way of the Plant Whisperer."

Nearly 3.5 billion years ago, long before humans were even a mere figment of Earth's imagination, the very first photosynthetic bacteria appeared on this planet. These first organisms were unlike any plants that you might find in your garden. These early organisms produced noxious sulfur and sulfate compounds.

Less than 3 billion years ago, these organisms evolved into something a little more familiar — cyanobacteria that produced oxygen. About one and a half billion years later, red and brown algae, and soon green algae, appeared on Earth's surface. As time passed, these early organisms began to evolve more complex cell structures, and species became more diverse.

Today, there are an estimated 400,000 plant species living on Earth. Every species has evolved dramatically from its bacterial ancestors, and the plants of today have the ability to perform complex functions not possible billions of years ago.

It has been known for years that plants can sense and respond to a variety of stimuli in nature. Plants certainly sense sunlight; any house plant owner knows that a plant will always grow towards a light source such as a nearby window. Plants also have an olfactory sense and can respond to smell. In a series of experiments at Pennsylvania State University with dodder vines and tomato plants, biologist Consuelo De Moraes demonstrated that the parasitic dodder vine uses scent to seek out a tomato plant to attach itself to.

Amazingly, it has also been proven that plants can hear. While it was once believed that ears were required to hear, many researchers now suspect that plants hear through some other means. An experiment was conducted by Heidi Appel, a chemical ecologist, where the sound of a caterpillar eating leaves was placed near a plant. In response, the plant began to release defensive chemicals in order to protect itself from the predator. In another fascinating demonstration, it was shown that a plant root would grow towards a buried water pipe that was dry on the exterior. The conclusion was drawn that the plant could hear the water flowing through the pipe.

Root trajectory experiments were even conducted by Charles Darwin who demonstrated how plants could detect light, gravity, moisture and pressure. Since the days of Charles Darwin, further research has revealed that plant roots can detect many other environmental conditions, including phosphate and nitrate levels. The most astounding part of these findings is that once a plant has collected information about gravity, pressure, phosphate levels and more, it must analyze this information and draw a conclusion. For example, the plant may use this information to decide which direction to lean or where to grow more roots in order to obtain more water.

A plant's ability to respond to the environment in such complex ways begs the question — do plants share the same awareness, consciousness, and intelligence that can be seen in many animal species that have also evolved over billions of years? Author Michael Pollan certainly believes that the line between plants and animals may not be so clear cut. In an experiment with bean plants, time lapse photography is used to more efficiently observe the movement of the plants. Pollan notes that time lapse photography is crucial because plants operate on a very different time scale than humans and other animals. Put simply, we are mobile while plants appear to be stationary. However, time lapse photography allows us to bring plants up to our speed.

In one demonstration, a bean plant is placed next to a pole. The tendril appears to thrash back and forth searching for a place to grip, and the leaves on the vine almost look strained and stressed. As the plant grows, it eventually reaches the pole and begins to wrap around and take hold. Once it has attached to the pole, the leaves start to look more relaxed and stress free. A certain consciousness seems to be present in the bean plant; the plant seems to be expressing feelings of stress, and later relaxation.

In another demonstration, two bean plants are used along with one pole. The two plants thrash around looking for a surface to latch on to. Eventually, one of the bean plants finds the pole and begins to take hold; the second bean plant is not so lucky. The second plant seems to give up on the pole once it has been "taken," and begins to thrash about in a different direction. This experiment reveals plant awareness; the second bean plant seems to be aware that the first has already claimed the pole.

The surprisingly close link between plants and animals is revealed in an experiment conducted by researchers involving a common house plant called a mimosa. Typically, the leaves of the mimosa will close up when they come in contact with an insect or other object. However, when a shot of ether is introduced, the mimosa leaves no longer close up when stimulated. Ether is a sedative used in humans; interestingly, it seems that this substance also works on plants. This experiment reveals a close tie between plants and animals; while plants do not have nerves, they still respond to ether in a similar way to humans.

The mimosa experiment is not the only evidence researchers have found that supports the idea that plants can feel. In an experiment conducted at the University of Freiburg, a plant is connected to a computer which measures electrical signals. When a single leaf of the plant is burned, an electrical spike can be seen on the computer. These results reveal why the ether from the previous example worked on the mimosa: the ether disrupts electrical signals while the flame creates electrical signals. Most notably, this two-part experiment reveals that the electrical signals which exist in animal cells also exist in plant cells. This suggests that plant cells could produce the same conditions found in animal cells that allow for intelligence, consciousness and pain reception.

As a reader, you may be feeling a little skeptical at this point—plants can analyze, feel and think? While these words may seem more appropriate for describing a human, or even a computer, it is this sort of personification that is getting many research-ers so excited. Despite plants' stationary life, it appears that they may possess many of the same qualities that make humans human.

*See Web Resources for a list of the online sources for this chapter.

Introduction

The Way of the Plant Whisperer

There are men and women across the planet quietly tending oversized English gardens or routinely harvesting massive vegetables and fruits. Their verdant house plants wildly thrive under the sparsest conditions, and the fecundity of plant growth on their watch borders on supernatural. They are nothing less than the crème de la crème of 'green thumbs.' Known as the plant whisperers, they are not only masters of the art of conscious plant care but also masters of the art of living.

If you long to have beautiful indoor plants and want to acquire the powers of the plant whisperers then you are in the right place! Discover the shocking truth about plant whisperers and learn their closely guarded secrets. Exposed here for the first time, you will learn:

* How observing your plants in a certain way can cause them to grow with wild abandon

*Why plants burst forth with thick, luxuriant growth when you treat them as individuals

* How plants effortlessly keep you and your family healthy

* How four simple laws of plant care can not only take your indoor garden to undreamt of heights of beauty but also transform your personal reality

*What is conscious plant care and why you shouldn't even consider getting a new plant without it

* How the sparsest plant can be transformed into a paragon of beauty when you apply these powerful grooming tips

*The right way to talk to your plants that makes them talk back the best way they know how — with profuse growth!

…and much, much more.

With these secrets under your belt, your indoor 'Garden of Eden' will be the envy of all your relatives, friends and neighbors. Everyone will want to know how you did it, but all you'll do is smile like a Cheshire cat. It's when they start begging you for solutions to their house plant failures that you will know your inner plant whisperer has been born.

Chapter One

How I Became a Plant Whisperer

I don't know about you, but I have always loved the idea of decorating my home with a collection of beautiful house plants. I love the look of flowing greenery hanging by the windows or enhancing side tables. All the better if they are in decorative pots. Nothing else, with the exception of original art, adds as much beauty and quality to a home, in my opinion. And not even expensive art serves as a silent testament to your life-giving, wholesome qualities as does the presence of one or more healthy, lush plants.

Bursting with primeval life force, healthy indoor plants not only raise the vibration (energy level) of an indoor space, but they also clean the air of pollutants, add the soothing, healing color green to the environment, and provide decorative, artistic shapes and textures to an ordinary tabletop or window frame. On the other hand, if plants are not well-groomed or in good health, marred by yellowing leaves, brown vines, scrawny fronds or a nearly bald 'crown,' they tell another story — one of neglect — and contribute low energy and subtle negativity to a space.

But sometimes even lovers of house plants like me, with all the best intentions, can't seem to make their dream of healthy house plants happen. Maybe your home gets very little outside light, or perhaps the air in your environment is extremely dry. You're not sure what the problem is, but all you know is that the formerly perky philodendron isn't growing, the dracaena marginata loses fronds daily, the ivy is wilting on the vine or the leaves on the pothos are turning yellow.

In my case, my initial lack of success with indoor plants led me to conclude I had a 'brown' thumb — maybe you've felt the same way. Let's face it, I 'killed' many a plant before turning a corner and discovering the unique method you will learn about in the pages of this book. When I used to look for answers to my house plant problems in books or on the internet, I usually found general advice about the light needs of a particular plant type, the moisture needs, the watering needs, etc. This information would help to a degree, but, to my chagrin, would not guarantee the health and beauty of my troubled plants.

Because following the experts' advice didn't always solve my plant problems and because so many of my plants looked unhealthy, I started to ponder how I could do a better job with my plants. At the same time, I wondered whether anything could be done at all, given the dry air and low light conditions of my home.

If you are anything like me, you too may have wondered what you're doing wrong, how you can solve the problem with your plant or plants, and whether the problem is even soluble given the environmental conditions in your home. Maybe you tried 'everything' and are ready to throw up your hands. Or maybe you're so busy and preoccupied that for all your good intentions, you don't have the time for what may seem like elaborate solutions suggested by the experts.

First, let me make it clear right now that I am an ordinary person just like you, not a trained expert in house plant care. I never took a course in the subject and have no degree in botany or horticulture. So why do I feel qualified to help you grow amazing house plants? Because my desire to have beautiful indoor plants led to my discovering a hidden gift, a gift that I have refined to a high degree — the gift of understanding the needs of my plants through my inner senses. Yes, it's true, I am a Plant Whisperer.

What is a Plant Whisperer? First, I will tell you what it is not — it is not really about whispering or talking to your plants, although you are welcome to talk and sing to them to your heart's content as plants love attention. But what it is about is using all of your senses to tune in to the needs of your plant. A plant whisperer has activated their innate ability to nurture plants.

What you need to know is that you too can become a plant whisperer. The ability to be sensitive to your plants in a way that enables you to care for them optimally can be learned, and that is what this book will teach you. Step by step, you will quickly and easily learn how to tune in to your plants like I did to increase their beauty, health and well-being. The process of doing so is fun and life-enhancing for you as well, so it works both ways.

You will love the results you get from developing sensitivity to the needs of your plants, as you watch them become greener, fuller, bigger and more beautiful. Gone will be the days of dead, dying or sick plants. You will know in an intuitive way what your plant needs and when. Much of the information presented in this material is simple, practical and obvious. But it is the combination of the practical and the intuitive that brings the extraordinary results.

Take note that this book is not a compendium of plant species with their pictures, names and general care instructions. In other words, you will not be given specific guidance on caring for various types of plants. You can easily find that information online, and I provide a Resources page that will help you with that. Instead we will begin by looking deeply at the nature of plants and their true purpose in your life. Then we will learn conscious plant care in all of its facets and identify the underlying factors that trigger healthy, profusely growing house plants. In the process, we will explore how to select an indoor plant and how to position it correctly in your home. We will look at how to illuminate, water, drain, feed, groom and cultivate your plants for maximum growth and beauty. At each juncture, we will expose the amazing, never-before-revealed inner secrets of plant health and growth — secrets that you will be applying when carrying out seemingly mundane plant care chores, so pay attention.

Last but not least, the information that follows requires an open heart and mind. Some of it may seem quite simple and obvious, while other parts may contradict everything you ever thought you knew about plants. So I recommend you just relax and allow the ideas to wash over you, rather than mentally argue with them to justify your existing beliefs. Allow the old and new ideas to co-exist. You don't have to accept or change anything. Just be willing to explore something new.

I guarantee that this will be a fun and unforgettable adventure that will forever alter your approach to plants, if you allow it to be. Not only will you expand your understanding of plants, but this information may also awaken a greater understanding of the nature of reality itself. Are you ready? I sure hope so because the train is leaving the station. All aboard, folks, let's go!

Chapter Two

Plants Speak, So Learn to Listen!

The first job of a plant whisperer is not to talk to your plants but to learn how to hear them speak! What, you say, plants speak? Yes, they do, and understanding how they communicate with you is the first step in creating your personal house plant heaven.

So how does a plant speak to you? In the only way they know how; by growing strong, luxuriant vines when they're 'happy' or by dropping leaves when they're 'sad,' by taking on the rich, green hue of their species or producing browning or yellowing leaves, by sending out perky and pliable growth or by wilting on the vine. Your first step is to understand that plants 'speak' to you through their body.

And the message conveyed is clear and specific, if only you can decipher its meaning.

While there are common messages that plants convey according to their species, through their leaves, vines, branches, and soil, house plants tend to be quite individualistic across species and often within as well. So, while each house plant may have general tendencies associated with their species, each one is unique enough—if only by virtue of their individual pot, soil, placement and size—to require your close attention to their condition and possible complaints. This is where most advice given by plant instructional manuals falls short. It is far too general to help you maximize your plant's potential. What is required is a more individualized approach—you need to determine what your plant is trying to tell you and then give it what it wants.

Let there be no mistake, we are the servants of our plants, not the other way around. Plants are living beings. By serving our plants well, they deliver health and beauty to our environment. It is an exchange, but it begins with you paying attention to your plants.

The primary purpose of this chapter is to introduce you to the idea that your plants communicate with you all the time and that it is your job to take note of what they are saying and then to attempt to give them what they want. Some of what you will be doing to satisfy your plant's needs will be experimental, as every plant is unique. Some of what you do is obvious, such as watering them or relocating them to a brighter spot. Flexibility is the name of the game, as you develop an intimate knowledge of your plants and their needs.

It all begins with respect — respect for the nature life forms expressing as plants. You have chosen to share your home with plant life and you are asking them to adapt to an unnatural condition — that of being indoors, confined to a pot and experiencing atmospheric conditions that are likely to be antithetical to their native environment. If this were your lot in life, you might complain too! We ask a great deal of our nature friends and should be grateful that plants adapt as well as they do, rather than get upset or offended by the problems they sometimes exhibit.

The truth is, indoor plants are eager to reward your care and attention with health and beauty, as they have an innate drive to live and express their potential as fully as possible. Your job is to note their condition by determining what optimal health looks like for them and what complaints they may be expressing. Many of these complaints can be healed or averted just by applying the basics of conscious plant care, which we will discuss in the following chapters. But first, in Chapter Three, we will take a look at plants with X-ray vision and ask the question—what is a plant, really?

Chapter Three

What Is a Plant, Really?

When I look at a house plant with everyday vision, a philodendron for example, I see a spontaneously growing assembly of vines, sporting green leaves and stems, that is embedded in and emerging from the surface of a pot of soil. Viewing plants in this way, some people may not even grasp that indoor plants are more than decoration, that they are, in fact, as alive as you and me. We are so used to seeing potted plants decorating living spaces, buildings and environments of all kinds, such as restaurants, plazas, offices, the lobbies of skyscrapers, homes, just about anywhere and everywhere, that we may have become desensitized to their essential reality as a living part of the nature kingdom, and, as such, a miraculous creation and gift of planet Earth.

It never hurts to take a moment to appreciate the miracle of a living plant. Not only is it a miracle, but it is also a mystery that penetrates to the very heart of existence. What is a plant, really? That is not an easy question to answer. If you can answer that question, you will have the key to understanding the source of all life.

Several years ago, I was fortunate to be given a window into the mystery of plants. As is my wont, I was doing an open-eye meditation in my living room one evening. For those who don't know, an open-eye meditation is a method of quieting the mind by focusing your attention on a wall or on an object in your environment. Any spot on the wall or object will do—and on this day, I stared at the wall opposite from where I was sitting. If you're a meditator, you know that the depth of your meditation varies from day to day and that sometimes you achieve what feels like a deeper or more powerful meditation. In those instances, you may feel the flow of higher energies surging through your being. This was one of those days.

As I stared at the wall, my mind empty of all distractions, the light in the dimly lit room intensified and objects began to blur, spontaneously transforming into waveforms that flowed past my field of vision.

Soon the contents of the entire room, up to and including its very walls, collapsed into lightwaves that grew brighter and brighter. My attention was drawn to my house plants, which had become churning patterns of light, each with their own unique waveform. Vines and fronds were transformed into licks of white fire as blindingly bright as lightning, and so alive, it was frightening!

In that moment, I experienced the primeval life force of plants and I realized that beneath the placid surface of each of the green potted plants that shared my home lurked a wild and irrepressible storm of nature.

So what is a plant, really? Try this technique yourself—activate your own 'X-ray vision.' I will leave you to draw your own conclusions.

In the following chapters, we will get into the nitty gritty of selecting and maintaining beautiful, healthy plants. We will explore the meaning and practice of conscious plant care and learn how to hone our powers of attention, intention, observation and allowance to ensure the well-being of our house plants.

Chapter Four

How to Select a Plant

Conscious plant care begins when you select a new plant for your home and continues throughout the plant's lifecycle. Before bringing home a new plant, you need to establish parameters. You need to know first of all, what kind of plant you want—a hanging plant, an upright plant, a floor plant? Will it be near a window or on a bookshelf? The type of plant you select depends on where you plan to situate it in your home and how much light that location receives. Don't underestimate how important this basic information is in finding a suitable plant that is likely to do well and be in harmony with its surroundings.

If you are unfamiliar with plants, then you might want to do some online research on the various types of house plants, or make the most of your garden store personnel, who often have a wealth of information and are happy to share it with you. Some easy to care for, low light plants to consider are spider plants, pothos, all philodendron varieties, dracaena palms, snake plants and nephthytis.

Sometimes it's more enjoyable to wander around a plant shop and see what catches your eye. When I am seeking a new plant, I usually begin by knowing the general parameters for the plant I want, and then I look for a plant that 'calls to me.' That is the way a plant whisperer chooses a new plant. In other words, I try to sense inwardly whether a specific plant is right for me and whether it is choosing me as much as I am choosing it. This recognition or lack thereof occurs in a split second. Making this type of connection with a plant gives me confidence that the plant will do well and inspires me to include it in my life.

Try the plant whisperer's selection technique as follows: determine the parameters for your plant ahead of time. Then empty your mind and focus only on the plants in your vicinity. Move around the store leisurely while your eyes lightly scan the assortment of plants. If there is a plant that is 'yours,' you will find yourself drawn to it. Mentally ask the plant if it wants to be yours. You will inwardly know the answer.

Next, there are a few practical measures to take before finalizing your decision. First, make sure, before you bring a plant home, that its need for light matches your environment. Second, inspect the leaves to make sure there are no signs of infestation or leaf damage. I also check the stems and soil to rule out bugs, slugs or fungus. In general, I look for a plant with full and balanced growth, one that appears to be as perfect as possible. A sloughing off of leaves is natural in the normal growth cycle of a plant, but plants with excessive browning, yellowing or other damage to their leaves should be put aside.

Don't be afraid to handle a plant and really get in there gently but firmly to examine it. The intimacy of touching a plant's body is part of the art of conscious plant care, and it should begin before you take the plant home. Explore the plant to make sure the leaves are healthy, the stems are firm and there is no damage to any part of the plant. If the plant is crying out for a bit of grooming, such as yellow leaves needing to be removed, just go ahead and remove them. Don't worry, the plant personnel will understand. What is left after your mini-grooming is a much better presentation of the plant you are considering taking home. Make your decision now, when it is looking its best.

Some garden center plants are already bursting out of their pot. So if you plan to repot your plant immediately, make sure that the soil you purchase for the new pot has excellent drainage. More information about soil can be found in Chapter Six. In general, the type of soil labeled 'palm and cactus' is often the best for most varieties. Soil that is treated to retain moisture may be tempting, but my advice is to resist. True, you won't have to water the plant as often, but be forewarned — the products added to moisture-retentive soil tend to attract fungal infestations and should be avoided.

In choosing a pot for repotting, go up no more than one to two sizes from the original, as that provides the best plant appearance and the best environment for optimal root growth. Too large a pot and the roots will grow excessively, drinking up all the moisture and stunting plant growth. At the same time, the plant will appear to be 'lost' in its pot. The goal is balance in all endeavors, most especially in conscious plant care.

In Chapter Five we will look at what to do after you bring home a new plant.

Chapter Five

Bringing Home Your New Plant

Y ou've brought your plant home, possibly along with a bag of soil and a bigger and prettier container. If the soil in your plant's original pot is dry, you need to repot the plant in the following way: water your plant thoroughly and wait one hour before you gently ease your plant out of the old pot and into the new. Water again and fertilize after repotting, remembering to drain thoroughly, and your plant will reward you with a trouble-free transition to the new pot.

If you plan to leave your new arrival in its original pot, then prepare your plant for your home by cleaning all of its leaves with a damp sponge, including topsides and undersides, water and fertilize if the soil is dry, and then place your new arrival in its chosen spot.

Plant shock is a common phenomenon with new plants. You bring home a beautiful, healthy plant, place it under good light and water and fertilize it faithfully, but the plant starts losing leaves and seems to be struggling.

This can happen for a number of reasons. Most likely your plant is going through a period of adjustment from the ideal conditions of the greenhouse, its original home, to the less ideal conditions of your home. Other possibilities include too much or too little light, too dry air, or too much or too little water and/or fertilizer. We will examine these possibilities one at a time.

If you've recently acquired a new plant, allow it time to adjust to its surroundings. Try not to overreact to any leaf shedding that may take place as it adapts to the new conditions. In more difficult transitions, this can be a prolonged affair that may cause you to fear the worst. But if you wait it out, the plant will rebound, albeit with perhaps smaller size leaves, but ultimately in a size and form that is better adapted for survival in your home.

When it comes to light, most house plants, with the exception of cactus and succulents, do not need direct sunlight, and will in fact overheat and dry out if placed in the path of sunlight. The majority of indoor plants enjoy indirect light and some can tolerate fairly low light conditions. Bright, indirect light is often the best exposure for indoor plants, supporting maximum growth without overtaxing the delicate plant structure.

Humidity supports lush plant growth, which is why greenhouses tend to be very humid environments. When you move a plant to your home, they may balk at the drier air by dropping leaves, and if near an open window, do the same when receiving drafts of cold air. This can be solved by keeping your plant away from an open window in cold weather and lightly misting the leaves once or twice per day to maintain moisture during the hot weather months.

We will devote an entire chapter to conscious plant care, including watering and fertilizing, but here we will mention that checking each individual plant's soil moisture level is critical in maintaining proper watering. That plus your awareness of each plant's needs through previous experience with that plant type, and/or careful observation, supports proper watering. Over watering should be avoided at all costs as it results in the yellowing of leaves and encourages fungal growth. Under watering results in browning of leaves and, if allowed to go on for too long, could cause permanent wilting and loss of all or part of the plant.

Regarding fertilizing, most plants need to be fertilized regularly in the growing season, but during the cold weather, may require no fertilizer or only light fertilizing. Be aware of these seasonal differences and act accordingly.

Maybe your plant is adjusting well, but you feel you don't have enough time to give it proper care, or you worry about keeping it as lush and healthy as when you first brought it home. In the next chapter, we will explore four quick and easy ways to support and maintain your plant's optimal health and beauty.

Chapter Six

The Four Building Blocks of a Plant's Life

W ater, sunlight, air, and soil are the building blocks of physical life on our planet and as such also comprise the essentials of life for plants. No plant growing on the surface of our planet will survive without air, soil, water or light. In this chapter, we will examine each of these elements and look at their practical applications to the conscious care of your plants.

Air

Air, as you know, is what we must breathe to survive as denizens of planet Earth. Like all living organisms, plants also need oxygen to survive. But in addition to utilizing oxygen during the process of respiration, they excrete oxygen back into the atmosphere. And when plants accumulate in large land masses, such as the Amazon Rain Forest, they contribute to a high percentage of the oxygen in the Earth's atmosphere. Without their function of absorbing carbon dioxide and excreting oxygen, life on Earth would quickly cease to exist.

Kept indoors, many plants are multi-taskers, effortlessly functioning as air cleaners, filtering mold, odors and other toxins from the atmosphere inside your home, while also maintaining their role as beautiful accent pieces to your home décor. How nice to know that the profusely growing philodendron which graces the wrought iron stand near the window in your breakfast nook is also a powerful anti-pollution device, silently serving you and your family 24/7.

When positioning a plant in your home, consider the air flow in that part of the house. Good air circulation enables optimal growth as it mimics the open air of nature. However, a cold draft from a nearby window can bring a halt to growth and cause potted plants to drop leaves, just as outdoor plants do during the cold weather months. On the other hand, a dry, airless space is totally unnatural and will cause plants to overheat and leaves to dry up.

To counteract this, they will require frequent watering and misting. Eventually, a plant can lose all of its leaves if it is not situated in the right location.

In general, plants love a warm, humid environment, so take that into consideration when preparing your home for plants. But if you live in a cold weather climate, rest assured that most house plants do adapt to an artificially heated home, particularly if you mist the leaves regularly to increase moisture in the more sensitive varieties, or raise the container on a dish filled with water and gravel. Just make sure that they continue to be kept warm as the outside temperature drops.

Soil

Certain species of plants grow in water and others in soil. But when we think of house plants, we typically picture a plant ensconced in a pot filled with soil. While there are indoor plants that grow hydroponically (in water or other nutrient solutions), that is not the purview of this book.

What is soil? In a nutshell, it is the top layer of the earth's surface. It absorbs water and other nutrients from the atmosphere and helps to support and grow plant life. Water and soil nutrients, which are primarily minerals such as carbon, nitrogen and phosphorus, are stored, transformed and cycled from the soil to the plant. Therefore, the quality of your plant's soil is critical if you want to have healthy plants.

The soil for your plant needs to be of a high quality. Ask your gardening center personnel to recommend the best type of soil. A premium mix usually works well as long as you avoid mixtures that have been treated with wetting agents to help retain moisture. That is a recipe for fungal growth. You want soil that contains both perlite and vermiculite, which encourage excellent drainage, as well as sphagnum peat moss and aged compost products.

When a plant sits in a pot, the nutrients in the soil tend to become depleted over time. They need to be replenished on a regular basis, hence the importance of fertilizer. There are many house plant fertilizers on the market. I get good results with the Miracle-Gro Liquid Houseplant Formula, found in many garden centers and hardware stores. However, be aware that fertilizers should not be used as frequently as the directions suggest, especially outside of the growing season.

If you notice a white crust accumulating on the top soil of a plant, you have over fertilized the plant. It means that your fertilizer has deposited excessive amounts of salt in the soil which has risen to the top. If allowed to remain there, it will block absorption of water and nutrients; so remove the areas with salt along with about one-quarter inch of soil and do not fertilize for several weeks. When you resume fertilizing, do so at one third the product's recommended frequency—unless it is prime growing season when you should fertilize regularly—but always keep an eye on how your plant is doing.

Water

Water is the most essential element for plants, and watering your plants correctly is the single most important thing you can do to maintain the health of your leafy friends.

Water enables nutrients to be transported from the soil to your plants, it maintains the rigidity that enables your plants to stand upright and it regulates the temperature of your plants. For these reasons, watering too little or too much can be fatal.

This is where conscious care is critically important. You need to develop sensitivity to the water needs of each and every one of your plants. This isn't as arduous a task as it sounds, as you will be applying your newly acquired skills of observation discussed in Chapter Nine, which will help you to determine when your plants need water.

The watering needs of plants vary according to the season, outdoor and indoor temperatures, plant species, and the size of the plant in relation to the pot, among other factors. For this reason, artificial schedules, such as "Water once per week," are a recipe for disaster.

First of all, before you water a plant you need to do a vision test — look at the soil under a good light, and if it looks dry, your plant most likely needs to be watered. Alternatively, try a touch test — put your finger in the pot and touch the top of the soil. If the soil feels dry, the plant needs water. If it feels damp or wet, in most cases you don't need to water. If it feels cold and you're not sure, dig your finger about one-half inch into the soil. If the soil feels damp below the immediate surface, most plants will not need watering yet, except for certain varieties that must be kept moist.

One of the most important things you can do to water your plant with the right frequency is to see how your plant reacts in the days before and after being watered. If a plant drops leaves, has wilted leaves or leaves that are browning at the edges, you may have waited too long to water it. Dropping leaves indicates that your plant may need watering right before it goes dry, so you will need to keep a close eye on it in the future. Browning leaf edges may signify a need for more humidity in the atmosphere, which can be solved by regular misting of the plant or by placing the pot on a dish with gravel and water.

On the other hand, if the plant needs to dry out before being watered, it will show yellow leaves shortly after being watered — perhaps one or two days later — in protest of being watered too soon.

Yellow leaves, however, can also be a sign of a plant needing water, because a leaf yellows before it dries up from lack of water and drops off. So if you haven't watered in a while and notice a yellow leaf, it's probably a sign that you need to water your plant. Just make sure to do the vision and/or touch test first.

Be aware that some plants, including cactus, succulents and some palms need to dry out completely or else will succumb to rot. In this case, check to see that the soil looks dry, but then also dig your index finger deep into the soil — two inches or more — and make sure it feels dry all the way down.

Once you water your plant, it is critical that the pot be allowed to completely drain off excess water before the plant is returned to its dish. Sufficient drainage is often the sole difference between a house plant that survives and thrives and one that dies. Be advised that you are signing your plant's death warrant if you allow it to sit in a watery dish, as it will quickly develop rot.

By observing your plants and using the vision and touch tests, you will eventually get to know the water needs of your plants, and keeping tabs on them will be like second nature. Nothing you do for your plants is more important than this. I suggest you reread this section and refer to it as often as necessary.

Light

Light plus chlorophyll enable your plants to carry out photosynthesis, which is a complex chemical process that, simply put, causes plants to turn carbon dioxide and water into carbohydrates and oxygen.

Using light energy, plants deliver oxygen to the planet and clean indoor air as mentioned earlier in this chapter. What is critical here is that each plant species has its own needs for light, and you must observe carefully to make sure that your house plant is not in danger because it is getting too little or too much light. And while you're observing, don't forget to turn your plants regularly so that they get even exposure.

Essentially, a happy plant is a plant receiving water and light according to its needs. The caretaker who masters an understanding of their plants' needs has become a plant whisperer whether they know it or not, as it takes conscious effort and a genuine love of plants to develop that understanding.

You'll notice that some plants, when moved from one location to another, seem to do significantly better or worse even when light and other factors appear to be equal. This mystery of placement can be observed over and over again. A plant whisperer understands that plants are sensitive creatures, responding to myriad environmental and energetic factors. Perhaps you spent more time admiring your plant when it was in a certain convenient location. It may then react to the loss of your attention energy (see Chapter 7) when left to its own devices in a different part of the house. The result—slower growth or loss of leaves.

At other times, a lackluster plant will grow like gangbusters when moved to a new spot, especially if it is in a location where you will notice it more. While it's possible that you may take better care of the plants within eyeshot than the ones out of sight, that is not the only explanation. When it comes to house plants, which must adapt to an indoor environment, there is often an unpredictable element. Sometimes, no matter how hard you try to provide the perfect conditions for your plants, they still present with problems. Sometimes they do much better than you ever imagined based on your experience with other plants of their species.

While most plants respond to conscious care, some are not always comprehensible, however much you strive to know them. Just be aware of this anomalous aspect of indoor plants and do the best you can.

Chapter Seven

The Law of Attention

The law of attention is the first secret of plant whisperers. It involves actively giving to your plants in a variety of ways. This is where plant whisperers get their reputation for "whispering." And it's absolutely true—plants thrive on attention, the kind of attention generated by being looked at, touched, spoken to or sung to, cared for physically, and even the attention sent by your thinking about your plant.

We give plants attention every time we water them, groom them, fertilize them, or simply look at them. When we open the curtains in the morning to let in the light that bathes our plants with life force, we are giving them attention. When we mist them on a hot summer's day, we are giving them attention.

As important as physical care is to your plant's well-being, there is another type of attention that plants thrive on, the kind that involves a subtle energy exchange between yourself and your plant. This energy exchange is a very real phenomenon based on scientific studies which have proven that plants react to human thought and human intention.

Using polygraph technology, scientists have determined that plants exhibit rudimentary emotional responses to the behavior of people around them, and even to their treatment of other plants in their vicinity. Research indicates that plants feel fear, for example, when approached with scissors, and react with pain when they or a sister plant are being cut. Research further indicates that plants in the wild respond in very sophisticated ways to ward off a predator. Because of the strength of accumulated research indicating that plants have consciousness, the country of Switzerland has recently passed a bill advocating for plant rights!

Few people know that house plants pick up on all energy directed toward them, both physical and nonphysical. The quality of the energy they receive is a function of its vibrational frequency. For example, positive, open, loving energy vibrates at a higher frequency than negative, closed, critical energy. The energy or vibrational frequency you direct to a plant through your thoughts, words and deeds evokes a positive or negative response in kind from the plant in the only way they know how to communicate—through their body via its health and appearance. This is one of the plant whisperer's most closely-guarded secrets.

Therefore, when you think or speak out loud positive thoughts about your plant—thoughts like, "How green you are; you are really filling in; your leaves are so soft and beautiful, etc."—you are giving your plant a powerful dose of positive attention. If all else is equal, your plant will reward you with faster growth, sturdy health and beautiful leaves. On the other hand, think or speak negatively about your plant and you are giving your plant negative attention, which is likely to result in slow or no growth and a generally mediocre appearance at best, disease at worst.

Negativity breeds ever more negativity if you look upon an unattractive plant and persist in criticizing or worrying about its appearance. Caught in a cycle of this type, there are only two things you can do. While continuing to provide conscious care, you can either attempt to break the cycle by appreciating your plant and visualizing it the way you would like it to appear —full, green, thriving and growing rapidly—or you can give the plant away.

That may seem harsh, but in my experience there is nothing in between. If a plant does not give you pleasure and you are not motivated to break the negative cycle through appreciation and visualization, consider giving it away. Life is too short to harbor in your living space something you are unable to love. Nor is it healthy for you to be distracted by an unhappy plant.

On the other hand, if you are motivated to keep visualizing your plant looking the way you would prefer it to, one of two things are likely to happen. The first is that the plant will visibly improve and become more like your image of it. The second is that you will find a solution to your plant's problem that enables it to heal and grow beautiful. This is the power of your attention when it is directed toward a positive goal—your plant will either respond to your positive visualization or your brain will direct your attention to the answer that you need.

All of your plants should evoke your love and each one should be a favorite for different reasons. If you can't clearly express why you love each one of your plants, you have not reached the depth of thought and feeling necessary for becoming a plant whisperer. You are a caretaker; that is all. And for some of you that might be enough, but I suspect that if you have read this far, you want to be more than just an ordinary caretaker of plants. If so, then read on to discover more secrets of the plant whisperers.

Chapter Eight

The Law of Intention

The law of intention is the second little-known secret of plant whisperers and is closely related to the law of attention. Intention as applied to your plants involves your overall goal with your plants. Your intention is your unspoken purpose in relation to your plants, including why you are interested in them and what you plan to do with them. For example, if you set your intention on having a beautiful indoor garden in your home, you are likely to find yourself an owner of this book!

How does this work? There is a part of the human brain known as the RAS (Reticular Activating System), otherwise known as the reticular formation, which functions like a homing device. It locks on to a passionate goal and almost magically guides your brain's attention to the resources and information in the physical world that will help you achieve that goal. When you set a strong intention to achieve a certain goal, your RAS causes you to focus on relevant information in your environment that you might otherwise ignore.

All of us have experienced the effects of our reticular activating system when pursuing everyday goals such as acquiring a new car. Once we determine what kind of car we want, we start to see it everywhere! That is the explicit function of our reticular formation — to connect us with our goal.

A strong intention is set by repetitively focusing on the goal, backed up with strong, positive emotion. For example, if you are desirous of brightening your home with a house plant Garden of Eden, your joyful image of beautiful foliage and overflowing plants will attract to you the information, resources, and methods for achieving that goal. All you need do is pay attention to your inspiration and motivation as it comes up, and pay attention as well to the signals in your outer world.

The reticular activating system directs us in two ways: externally, through real world information that reaches our awareness, and inwardly, through inspiration and motivation arising in your mind as thoughts, ideas or impulses. Follow the external information and your thoughts and impulses to their logical conclusion, and you will find answers to your questions.

If your question is how to best fertilize your house plants, the answer will arise through something you see or hear. It could appear via something as mundane as the results of an internet search or as esoteric as the urge to mix certain chemicals together and create your own fertilizer. Your part in fulfilling an intention includes expecting to receive the answer as you go about your business, and taking note of what transpires. If you stay alert, the answer will come into your awareness in one way or another, and when it does, as it will, your final job is to simply apply it.

The law of intention allows you to set goals and receive guidance from external and internal sources to help you achieve those goals. In the next chapter we will explore the third most closely-guarded secret of plant whisperers.

Chapter Nine

The Law of Observation

T he law of observation is the third secret of the plant whisperers. You may recall that the first secret, the law of attention, is primarily a mode of giving to plants through your appreciation and care. While an energy exchange occurs in any interaction with plants, and attention cannot be entirely divorced from observation, the law of observation is primarily a mode of receiving; you empty yourself and open to receive from your plants.

Observation strengthens your psychological connection with your plants. The purpose of this connection is to maximize your enjoyment of plants and assure their optimal development.

There are three forms of observation: plant gazing, plant studying and plant telepathy.

Plant Gazing

A plant whisperer will gaze often at their plants when they are at home. For example, if they are in the living room reading a newspaper, they will periodically look up and simply allow their eyes to sweep over the plants in their vicinity, receiving information, pleasure or satisfaction from their green hue or their variegated leaves, their interesting forms, their overflowing growth; whatever there is to notice or enjoy about your plants is experienced in the gaze.

Gazing occurs at a distance, yet it enables you to receive an energy flow of serenity, beauty and healing from your plants' colors and shapes, as well as from their primal life force. It is also a way of quickly checking on their condition, as gazing may also inform you, almost subliminally, that your plants need water or have some other need.

While it is impossible to gaze at your plants without also giving them energy, the higher purpose of the gaze is to empty yourself and be receptive to their energy flow. Ultimately, the gaze assures a positive flow of energy and communication between the plant whisperer and their plants. Plants reward your gaze with verdant growth, so gaze often and lovingly at your plants, knowing that your gaze is like manna to your leafy friends.

Plant Studying

This second form of observation means exactly what it says. This is the kind of observation where you are seeking information by looking closely at a plant, perhaps inspecting the leaves or the soil. The purpose of plant studying is mostly to determine its condition and whether your plant is receiving the right kind of care. You should always use close observation before watering a plant, repotting it, grooming it, or moving it to a new location. But sometimes, you study a plant just because you enjoy the intimate contact, the exquisite design or texture of its leaves, the presence of new growth.

Plants thrive on being studied, and will tend to give you more of whatever you note about them, as if they can literally read your mind. For this reason, plants should never be treated as if they were inanimate objects. They must always be given the respect life deserves.

Plant Telepathy

If a plant continues to struggle despite your close observation, there is one failsafe method — the ultimate tool on a plant whisperer's toolbelt — and that is plant telepathy. Yes, that's right. Simply ask your plant what it needs, silently or out loud. Then be quiet and listen! Within your own mind the response will form in words, or perhaps, as an image. Then you must step out on faith and act on that information.

I have one plant whose watering needs remain a mystery, despite my best efforts to observe and understand it. So I literally ask it if it needs water. Inwardly, I wait to hear a 'yes' or 'no' before watering. Your plant will tell you what it needs, if only you take the time to ask and then open to receive its response.

Observe your plants from a distance and close-up to fine-tune their care or just to enjoy them. Communicate with them telepathically as needed, and take action accordingly. If you follow these practices you will optimize your plants' health and well-being. As always, it's a two-way street in which you can expect to receive greater peace and serenity the closer you become to your plants.

Chapter Ten

The Law of Allowance

Plant whisperers practice the law of allowance in all things, including their relationship with their plants. What is the law of allowance and what form does allowance take in regard to plants?

Allowance refers to letting things be as they are. To quote spiritual teacher Satyam Nadeen, "What is, as is." When applied to plants this has many meanings, including the acceptance of the appearance, structure and rate of growth of your plants, the needs and problems of your plants, and a willingness to work with their natural tendencies, rather than to try to bend them to your will.

It means allowing a plant to grow the way it grows, to look the way it looks and to require whatever it requires. While this may sound obvious, many people are not fully aware of the inherent aliveness of plants and believe that house plants exist to please them. They have a controlling attitude toward their plants and want to beat them into shape — prune them within an inch of their lives, over feed with fertilizer or hormones to force growth, leave them to 'decorate' poorly lit or ventilated areas of a home as if they were inanimate objects, or worst of all, totally neglect them. This, of course, will never work, as nature is simply what it is and can only be itself at all times.

Plant whisperers, on the other hand, act as servants of their plants, not as their masters. They seek to determine what their plants are telling them and to respond in a way that meets their needs. Plant whisperers adopt a supportive and experimental stance, always working with their plants, always asking themselves how they can better assist their plants to achieve optimal health and beauty.

Plant whisperers let the appearance of a plant follow its natural tendencies, including growth, shape, color and style. Each plant is so different, even within the same species. They grow and fill the pot in their own way, every leaf as unique as a snowflake. The plant whisperer appreciates and recognizes these differences, and seeks to enhance 'what is,' rather than trying to turn the plant into something it is not.

Plants can sense this non-resistant approach, this deep acceptance by their caretaker, and they respond with greener color, faster growth and greater overall health. What they are reacting to is the vibration of acceptance, which is a form of love that liberates. Set free to be what they already are, plants feel safe in your presence and that sense of safety opens the door for their greater self-expression.

Chapter Eleven

The Art of Plant Grooming

One of the delights of a plant whisperer's life is the act of grooming their plants. Why do we love to groom our plants so much? Because we love making our plants more beautiful and we enjoy the peaceful feeling we get from the close physical contact.

Plants emit a calming, soothing energy that communicates to anyone spending time with them, especially when touching and caring for them. Not only does a plant whisperer directly benefit from plant grooming with an enhanced sense of calm and well-being, but they also reap the benefits of having more beauty to drink in when plant gazing at home.

You may be wondering why plants need to be groomed. After all, millions of plants in the wild live naturally and grow freely, so why not house plants? Actually, plants in the wild are a whole other kettle of fish. They are subject to all manner of damage and disease, yet they grow abundantly because of their sheer volume, because of their ability to adapt to conditions, and because their environment automatically provides for them.

On the other hand, indoor plants are totally dependent on you for survival. Grooming is a survival tool that assists plants to maintain health while facilitating faster and fuller growth. It is also an aesthetic tool that enables plants to look more attractive in your home.

Grooming involves three fundamental practices, cleaning, untangling and pruning. We clean to remove dead leaves and accumulated dust and grime, we untangle to improve a plant's appearance and support its growth, and we prune or cut back to encourage top growth and a fuller appearance.

Cleaning, Untangling and Pruning

Plants shed leaves and become dusty over time. They may also grow in an unruly fashion if left to their own devices. To keep your plants beautiful and suitable for your home, they need to be cleaned, untangled and trimmed, just like your pets.

A good time to groom your plants is when you water them. Take your plant to the sink, gently spray or rinse the leaves, water the soil thoroughly and then go through the leaves or fronds of your plant, untangle leaves and vines so that they fall freely, remove any yellow or brown leaves, and trim any leaves that are only slightly damaged or browning a bit at the edges. I like to run my fingers through the fronds of my palm trees. It separates each frond and spruces them up, giving them a 'big hair' appearance.

With vine-growing plants, make sure that some of the vines have not ended up on the wrong side of the pot because they got tangled up or because someone forced them there to fill a lighter area. Following the law of allowance, a plant whisperer always lets vines fall naturally and does not attempt to manipulate a plant's appearance. House plants appreciate that, as it puts less stress on their leaves, stems and roots when vines are allowed to drape the side of the pot that is closest to where they are growing. Ultimately, plants look better and grow better when you follow this rule.

The next step is to prune your plant by pinching new growth at the tips to encourage more growth at the top of the plant, or take cuttings when uneven growth in certain parts of the plant gives it an unbalanced appearance.

This is also a good time to add more top soil to the pot if the soil level looks low. Potting soil tends to erode over time, eventually exposing the plant's roots if it is not periodically replenished. Soil should fill a container to about one-half inch from the top.

One of the big advantages of washing the leaves is to avoid gnats, those tiny flying bugs that hover around your plant's leaves. If you already have gnats, water goes a long way in getting rid of them; they can usually be dispelled simply by washing the leaves and keeping them clean. Many other types of bugs and diseases can be prevented by periodically washing the leaves. But in general, indoor plants, if carefully selected in the way we describe in Chapter Four, are not nearly as vulnerable to affliction as outdoor plants and can be easily managed with these simple techniques.

I like to do something for my plants that I call 'rain,' which is to place them in the sink and run a fairly strong flow of room temperature water over the leaves to mimic rain in nature, which is their native means of receiving water. Plants should always be watered or cleaned with room temperature water, meaning neither hot nor cold, but as close as possible to the temperature of rain in summer.

Be aware that anytime you handle plants, there is a chance of damaging them. This occurs most often during grooming, so try to work as carefully and gently as you can. If you have accidentally torn a leaf or even broken a vine, do what the plant whisperers do. Say "I'm sorry," out loud to your plant. Your plant is likely to be feeling fear and pain and will be soothed by your voice. You can then use the broken portion as a cutting if a node is available.

To water and groom a plant, all the equipment you need is a watering can, a spray container for misting leaves on hot days, a pair of scissors, a bag of soil, and a dedicated container (such as a glass or mug) for your cuttings. You might want to also keep on hand some pebbles or gravel, so that you can put a pot, with a plant needing more humidity, on a raised bed of gravel and water.

Taking Cuttings

Plant whisperers know that plants have feelings and, therefore, they behave compassionately to their plants. When approaching to take cuttings, they speak reassuringly to them. If they accidentally knock into a potted plant but catch it before it falls, they will apologize to the ruffled plant and speak soothingly to it as if it were a frightened child.

Cuttings should be taken from plants in the areas where growth is uneven or excessive to create pleasing balance and conformation. Another good place to take a cutting is where a vine has become thin due to dropped leaves and there is one or more leaves at the end of the vine but little else until higher up towards the top. You would then cut the vine right below the uppermost leaf and use the bottom leaves with several inches of stem as your cutting.

Cuttings are trimmed at one-quarter to one-half inch below the last node and then placed in a small container filled with water until roots begin to form. The water in the cuttings container should be changed every three days or so to keep it fresh and to prevent rotting of the stem in the place where the plant was cut.

It is also wise to check the end of your cutting stems when you change the water, and trim off any appearance of rot. If you do so, the majority of the cuttings should continue forward to grow roots and plant successfully. While a small percentage of cuttings may rot all the way up to the last available node and must be discarded, and others may die in the cuttings container or refuse to grow roots, you can expect at least nine out of ten cuttings to survive and grow.

Roots develop more quickly during the growing season or when the atmosphere is hot and humid. If the weather's warm, they might appear in three days, as opposed to weeks during the cold weather. So be patient and allow the cuttings to take as much time as needed to develop roots. Placing the cuttings in a warm spot, such as near a lamp, may help the process along in the cold weather. You can experiment with this, but I would advise against putting delicate cuttings under intense indoor lights or sunlight. Indirect light and room temperature is usually sufficient to develop cuttings.

When roots are approximately one-quarter inch in size or more, cuttings are ready to be planted. Take a wooden chopstick or similar utensil and make a good size hole in the soil, going down one-half to one inch or more depending on the size and weight of the cutting. The hole is made deeper when it needs to support more weight. Gently place the roots and lower stem of the cutting into the soil and use your utensil to help press the stem and roots deep into its hole for greater stability. Fill in the hole all around the stem with soil and gently pat it down.

The cutting should be stable and upright. Then gently water and fertilize the soil around the cutting. The majority of cuttings, well over 90%, will take if you use this method.

One of the great joys of grooming plants is your ability to increase their fullness, and greatly improve their appearance, by planting cuttings in the soil. The top of a plant tends to lose the most leaves over time, eventually giving it a sparse or even bald appearance in the area where the plant meets the soil. This can be completely counteracted by regularly adding cuttings back to your plant. You will be well-rewarded by a beautiful, thick, lush plant, with a full head of 'hair.'

Another use of cuttings is to grow a completely new plant. Plant whisperers do this all the time, and enjoy raising plants from small cuttings to maturity. If you have sufficient cuttings from one plant species, then by all means plant them in a pot as the foundation for a whole new plant. To get the best result, start planting in the dead center of the pot and then continue to plant in ever-widening circles as you gradually work your way to the pot's outer edge. Over time, you can fill in the pot as more cuttings become available, then just apply conscious care and enjoy your beautiful new plant! I make a practice of giving one cutting back to the mother plant for every eight or ten I give to its 'satellites.' It only seems fair.

Chapter 12

How to Talk to Your Plants to Make Them Grow

I'm sure you'll agree that no book by a plant whisperer would be complete without step by step instructions on how to talk to your plants! But we won't tell the neighbors we do this, will we? Shh. Let's just keep it between you and me.

We know plants love attention—physical and metaphysical. They respond to your touch, your intentional care, your observation and your visualization of their health and beauty. But talk to your plants? That's a joke, isn't it? If you do it you must be crazy.

The truth is, plant whisperers talk to their plants all the time. We whisper, we hum, we sing, we soothe and, most importantly of all, we speak both silently and out loud to our beloved green friends. These communications, however, are purposeful and of two distinct types. The first is to help them grow and stay healthy. The second is to heal ourselves.

Did you say 'heal ourselves'? This second type of communication may appear so surprising and esoteric to some people, I hesitate to even mention it here and, in truth, it is not in the purview of this book to discuss self healing through plant intelligence and plant consciousness. But keep an eye out for my new groundbreaking book, which is coming soon, entitled "Your Houseplant Speaks!: How to Use Your Favorite Indoor Plant as a Therapist." It will show you exactly how it's done!

Getting back to the first type of communication: how do we speak to plants to encourage their growth and health? There are four methods and we will take a look at each one.

Compliment Your Plant

Plants love compliments. When we pass by one of our houseplants, and if we feel inspired, we may caress a leaf and say, "How beautiful you are." Just doing this tends to sustain and increase the beauty of your plant, for, as mentioned in Chapter Eight,

"The Law of Intention," what we focus on multiplies.

A plant is a living spirit that reacts to your tone, to the intent of your message and, at some level, to your words. It has the ability to understand instinctively what you are asking of it, and tends to give you what you ask for. The more we admire our plants out loud, the more they respond over time with increased growth and loveliness.

Reassure Your Plant

An even more important, foundational technique for talking to your plants is the practice of reassurance. House plants are dependent on you for their survival and need to sense that they will be looked after and are safe. This is not understood literally from your words but from your energetic intent when speaking words of reassurance to them.

Simply let them know when you water them, groom them, or study them, "I will take care of you. You're safe and can grow. I will always take care of you. See, I'm taking care of you right now and will continue to."

Or if you notice one of your plants needs water as you're about to leave the house, just say to it, "I will water you later. Don't worry. I will take care of you." Your soothing words land on the plant's energy field, where your intent is felt and understood on some level. It will help the plant wait a bit longer without needing to send you more serious signs of dehydration.

Tell Your Plant What to Do

In this third and most interesting technique for helping your plants grow and stay healthy, you ask them to grow for you, to give you more leaves, more flowers, more of whatever it is you desire from them within reason. This is especially helpful when they've become dormant after some kind of shock, such as being dropped, transplanted, or over-pruned. You can be very specific in your request, just get ready to be amazed.

For example, you can say to your dormant plant, "Grow more leaves. I want you to always be generating five new leaves or more. I will take care of you and in exchange I ask that you have five new leaves or more growing at any given time." We always add 'or more' so that we avoid limiting our plant's growth in case it wants to give us more than five leaves. Not long thereafter, you will start to see new leaves appear on your plant!

If the new growth is not the amount specified then say to it, "Thank you for the three new leaves that are coming up, but I want at least two more. Give me two more please." Persist in asking for more, and soon you will see two new leaves emerging from your plant. All you need is a little patience, as plant time is not human time.

It is also essential to speak to your plant when you may have pruned it excessively with all the best intentions. You can't help noticing that your plant looks droopy, as if it were bereft. In fact, what happened is that your over-pruning upset the delicate balance of the plant's energy field and it is struggling to rebalance itself. In this instance, you must apologize to your plant. Say, "I am so sorry for cutting off so much of you. It was a mistake and I won't do it again. I will take care of you. You're safe now, so please grow for me. You're going to be okay." In time, the plant will start to fill out again and look stronger.

Pose a Question to Your Plant

Not only do plant whisperers apologize to their plants for accidents or mistakes, but as mentioned in Chapter Nine, "The Law of Observation," we also ask our plants questions when we feel unclear as to what is wrong with them or what they need. In this fourth technique, we pose a question mentally or verbally to our plant, and then listen for a telepathic response.

Plants do 'speak' to us if we pay attention, and not only through their apparent health or lack thereof, but also with actual words or images sent telepathically. What this means is that the plant understands the intent of your question and attempts to tell you what you need to know. We need not debate here whether you are simply accessing your own subconscious mind, which registers data that the conscious mind cannot perceive, or are actually 'hearing' the instructions from your plant. Try to suspend judgment and just tune into your plant.

This technique works best if you get into a quiet, meditational state, then pose the question to your plant mentally or verbally and wait in silence to allow the answer to arise within your mind. The answer will appear as words or pictures, although in some instances, it may come to you at a later time, either through new information received from the outer world or from within. This is always a valuable technique to use when you need extra help in caring for your plant

Chapter Thirteen

Practicing the Secrets

I n this chapter, we look at how plant whisperers apply the laws of attention, intention, observation and allowance on a daily basis to practice their trademark conscious plant care.

When an ordinary person goes into a plant store to find a new plant, they most often buy on impulse and hope for the best. On the other hand, plant whisperers follow the law of intention by deciding in advance exactly what size, shape and type of plant they are seeking. They then allow themselves to be drawn to the right plant by their inner senses; a plant will in some way "speak" to them. They do this to ensure that their new house plant is in harmony with them and their environment.

At home with their new plant, a plant whisperer follows the basics of conscious plant care by providing high quality soil, the right size pot, and by situating the plant in a spot where it is given sufficient light and warmth. The plant is then watered and fertilized according to its needs. Using the law of observation, the plant is closely observed on an ongoing basis to see if care is needed or to note if adjustments to its care should be made.

The law of observation also includes plant gazing to enjoy their beauty, plant studying to build a deeper connection and plant telepathy to communicate directly with your plant.

At home, plant whisperers give and receive energy from their plants through the law of attention. They help maintain their plants' peak health through their thoughts, by visualizing their plant's well-being, through their words, by speaking to plants with appreciation and admiration, through music, by singing to plants or playing beautiful music, and through their timely care. The law of attention is closely related and works in tandem with the law of observation.

In following the law of allowance, plant whisperers seek to understand and work with, not against, the essential nature of each plant, its growing cycle, personal style and needs. They regularly groom their plants by cleaning, untangling and pruning, so that they look their best and are protected from disease. Cuttings are taken, cultivated, and then replanted to increase fullness or counteract the loss of leaves at the top of a plant. All the while, plant whisperers maintain a delicate balance between helping a plant adapt to its environment and allowing it to be its natural self.

Through the four laws of attention, intention, observation and allowance plant whisperers accept plants as they are—alive, imperfect, magnificent, and occasionally resistant to even the most sophisticated care.

Plain and simple, a plant whisperer loves their plants no matter what, and finds great joy in tending their indoor garden.

Conclusion

Kudos to the New Plant Whisperer

You have done the work, walked the walk, mastered the skills and achieved a goal that most will never achieve in their lifetime. It took your dedication plus the specialized knowledge in this book. Now congratulate yourself on becoming a plant whisperer with beautiful indoor plants that will enhance your life and bring you pleasure forever.

But get ready—creating an indoor plant Eden also has some unexpected side effects. People will usually gasp when they come into your home like they do when they enter mine. They will exclaim how beautiful your plants are, how green, and often they will ask you how you did it. When you try to explain, their eyes may go blank because it can be hard for them to comprehend the simple, yet powerful work of a plant whisperer.

Another type of 'friend' — usually the sour, the cynical and/or the most envious of all — will roll their eyes at this display of plant fecundity, thinking, if not saying out loud, that it is "too much." In the presence of these sour grapes, let the negative energy roll off your back and understand what it is they are really reacting to. They feel inadequate in the face of your obvious ability to cultivate and magnify life in the form of plants!

And never forget that your leafy friends will reward you for giving them the loving care they so richly deserve, in the only ways they know how — by growing abundantly, cleaning your air, soothing your spirit and quietly filling your living space with beauty. Better than an even exchange, I'd say!

Before you go, please don't forget to get your special gift, the two-volume starter library, "The Art of Bonsai" and "A Beginner's Guide to Organic Vegetable Gardening." Just think, now you can apply the secret knowledge you acquired from *Secrets of the Plant Whisperer* to growing beautiful bonsai trees or tasty organic vegetables!

To receive your free gift, send an email to info@diamondstarpress.com with your purchase receipt and 'Send Plant Whisperer Gift' in the subject field, and we will get your free gift out to you right away. Do it now before you forget!

Did You Enjoy This Book?

Dear Reader,

Thank you for reading "Secrets of the Plant Whisperer: How to Care for, Connect, and Communicate with Your House Plants."

My purpose in writing this book was twofold: to help my readers have gorgeous, healthy house plants and to inspire them with a greater appreciation for the precious natural world of planet Earth by revealing the deeper reality of the beautiful plants that live inside our homes.

If you would like to recommend this book to other readers, please write a brief review on Amazon. It will only take a few minutes of your time, and it will really help me to reach more readers who will discover this book thanks to your review.

Thanks again, and wishing you the very best!

S. F. Howe

Web Resources

Plant Websites

Plant Care Site—Comprehensive indoor and outdoor plant website with an indispensable Plant Encyclopedia that will allow you to set detailed criteria for researching indoor plants.
Go to http://www.plantcare.com/

Air Purifying Plants—15 house plant varieties that are scientifically proven to clean air.
Go to http://air-purifier-reviewsite.com/blog/15-house-plants-you-can-use-as-air-purifiers/

Gardeners Forum—Popular site for both outdoor and indoor gardeners.
Go to http://www.agardenersforum.com/

Books and Other Media

The Secret Life of Plants by Peter Tompkins and Christopher Bird—A classic of its kind and one of the first books exploring the scientific evidence for the physical, emotional and spiritual relationship between plants and humans.

Go to http://www.amazon.com/, select the Books category and enter 'The Secret Life of Plants' into the Search field.

Music for Plants—Research has shown that plants especially love violin selections by Bach. Go to: http://www.amazon.com/, select the Music category and enter 'Bach violin concertos' into the Search field.

Plant Products

Indoor Plant Stands—A wide selection of attractive and useful plant stands for every room in the house. Go to http://www.amazon.com/, select the Patio, Lawn & Garden category and enter 'indoor plant stand' into the Search field.

Plant Grow Lights—A great choice of Grow Lights and Miniature Greenhouses for every indoor gardening need. Go to http://www.amazon.com/, select the Home & Kitchen category and enter 'plant lights' into the Search field.

Plant Containers and Accessories—Attractive pots in a variety of styles and sizes.

Go to http://www.amazon.com/, select the Plant Containers & Accessories category and enter 'planters and pots indoor' into the Search field.

Miracle-Gro Liquid Houseplant Food—This is the best general fertilizer for house plants. Go to http://www.amazon.com/, select the Home & Kitchen category and enter 'miracle-gro liquid houseplant food' into the Search field.

Additional Sources

* Online Sources for the *Preface*: **Science and Plant Intelligence**.

http://www.scientificamerican.com/article/do-plants-think-daniel-chamovitz/

http://www.pachamama.org/blog/do-plants-have-consciousness

https://answersingenesis.org/biology/plants/the-origin-of-plants/

http://www.scientificamerican.com/article/timeline-of-photosynthesis-on-earth

http://www.npr.org/sections/krulwich/2012/05/24/153583873/do-plants-smell-other-plants-this-one-does-then-strangles-what-it-smells/

https://www.bgci.org/policy/1521/

http://www.pri.org/stories/2014-01-09/new-research-plant-intelligence-may-forever-change-how-you-think-about-plants

https://www.collective-evolution.com/2015/05/15/do-plants-respond-to-pain-scientists-conduct-an-experiment-to-find-out/

http://www.sciencedirect.com/science/article/pii/S1002007109000161

http://www.newyorker.com/magazine/2013/12/23/the-intelligent-plant

Books by S. F. Howe

MIND · BODY · SPIRIT

PLANT INTELLIGENCE

Secrets Of The Plant Whisperer: How To Care For, Connect, And Communicate With Your House Plants

A plant whisperer reveals the hidden truth about plants and why relating to them in a conscious way is vital for their health and well-being. Available in print and digital editions.

Your Plant Speaks!: How To Use Your House Plant As A Therapist

Let your house plant solve your problems! Discover the little known art of receiving life coaching from your favorite plant. *Coming Soon!*

HIGHER CONSCIOUSNESS

Matrix Man: How To Become Enlightened, Happy And Free In An Illusion World

The author reveals a new reality paradigm that can liberate you from the limiting beliefs and programs that prevent a joyful and fulfilling life. Available in print and digital editions.

The Top Ten Myths Of Enlightenment: Exposing The Truth About Spiritual Enlightenment That Will Set You Free!

Essential reading for spiritual seekers. What no one else will tell you to help you avoid the many pitfalls of the spiritual journey. Available in print and digital editions.

The Bringer Discourses: On Waking Up To The Mind Control Programs Of The Matrix Reality

For those seeking freedom from cultural indoctrination, this book offers a higher dimensional perspective on the most ingrained and unquestioned aspects of everyday life, and has the ability to heal and awaken humanity. Available in print and digital editions.

PERSONAL GROWTH

Vision Board Success: How To Get Everything You Want With Vision Boards!

A powerful technique for achieving goals and manifesting your desires. Available in print and digital editions.

Sex Yoga: The 7 Easy Steps To A Mind-Blowing Kundalini Awakening!

A technique for activating the chakras to induce a powerful kundalini experience. Available in print and digital editions.

Morning Routine For Night Owls: How To Super-charge Your Day With A Gentle Yet Powerful Wake-up Routine!

Morning rituals aren't only for morning people, and they don't have to be rough and tumble or performed at top speed to set up a perfect day. Welcome to the world of the gentle yet powerful wake-up routine for night owls! Available in print and digital editions.

CONSCIOUS HEALTH

When Nothing Else Works: How To Cure Your Lower Back Pain Fast!

The simple method that no doctor will ever tell you about. Requires no drugs, no surgery, and no special equipment. Available in print and digital editions.

Transgender America: Spirit, Identity And The Emergence Of The Third Gender

A higher consciousness perspective on the transgender agenda and why it is being rolled out at breakneck speed to social engineer a gender dysphoria epidemic. Available in print and digital editions.

About the Author

S F. Howe is a plant whisperer and transformational psychologist who has made noted contributions to the literature of higher consciousness and self healing.

In "Secrets of the Plant Whisperer: How to Care for, Connect, and Communicate with Your House Plants," the author aims to raise spiritual awareness of the true nature of plants by teaching you how to tune into your house plants to increase your own and your plants' health and well-being. By learning this method of conscious plant care, which combines the practical with the intuitive, you will not only master the art of plant care, but also the art of living.

For more information, please visit https://amazon.com/author/sfhowe

Made in the USA
Middletown, DE
19 December 2020